LIGHT

A Book of Poems

Jan Marquart

Jan Marquart
Copyright © 2018
Texas

ISBN: 978-0-9973308-6-1

Other Books by the Author

Write to Heal

The Mindful Writer, Still the Mind, Free the Pen

The Basket Weaver, a Novel

Kate's Way, a Novel

Echoes from the Womb, a Book for Daughters

Voices from the Land

The Breath of Dawn, a Journey of Everyday Blessings

How to Write from Your Heart (booklet)

How to Write Your Own Memoir (booklet)

A Manual on How to Deal with a Bully in the Workplace

A Writer's Wisdom

Unveil the Wounded Self, a Guided Journal for PTSD Sufferers

Never Too Late, a Novel

Cracked Open, a Book of Poems

Children's Books

Can You Find My Love? Series of 10 educational books

∞

We may encounter many defeats but we must not be defeated.

Maya Angelou

∞

Dedication

I dedicate this book to all poets who write verses in their minds and hearts but never put their words, images, dreams, inspirations, or life experiences on the blank page.

I encourage them all: *write!*

To me a book is a message from the gods to mankind; or, if not, should never be published at all.

Aleister Crowley

Acknowledgment

I would like to take this time to acknowledge some of the poets who widened my view of the world. This list is far from all-inclusive:

Mary Oliver
Edgar Allen Poe
W. S. Merwin
Rainer Maria Rilke
Maya Angelou
W. H. Auden
Jimmy Santiago Baca
Ellen Bass
Kahlil Gibran
Sylvia Plath
William Stafford
Dylan Thomas
Norman Hansen

Bygone Days

Another family lives there now

filling the air with aromas

from their recipes

in the narrow blue

kitchen where I once washed dishes

and placed them in the dish drainer

while mom dried them with a

linen towel near a built-in

sideboard. Its floor made of tiny

blue and white octagon-tiles.

Those were the days – weren't they?

The days of fine details

by care and skill.

I wonder if the family there

love those details as much as I did?

I wonder if they have removed them thinking

modern is better?

        Frosted windows

            carved moldings

                tiny octagon-tiled floor.

I loved that house.

I let my mind

return there

anytime I want.

I love to go home.

∞

Chance

Flames of hot orange shoot

to earth

streaking the wide land with

a new morning as

birds begin their songs of praise

      flap their wings

            soar wildly.

Be free -

they teach.

Today is another chance.

∞

City Kids

Brick stoops

concrete walls

send kids to

    parks

        to lay on sweetened grass

            from morning dew.

Their young spirits

enjoy nature's treats

as the scent of a new day

marks the memory of

their lives.

While they dream

the night skies

    replete with angels

announce

the stars are there to

prove the light in their souls.

∞

Don't Push

Don't push me out of

my pain -

it is my gift

to birth wisdom.

Graduation Day

Applause and cheers
by families and friends
rocked the room for each student
who walked across the stage.

My name finally called
I walked with great excitement onto the
stage - the first in my family
to get a four-year degree as
my blue flowered chiffon dress
flowed gracefully with each step -
its darts taken in to
fit my flat chest.

But my walk across the stage
was met with cutting silence.

I stopped, turned, and
faced the silent crowd
frantically waving

18

pretending my family was there

    smiling

        tears in their eyes

           so proud of me.

The silence remained deafening.

Eventually

a single clap broke the stillness,

then another came from

the back of the room.

Then -

    silence so brutal it

        hurt my ears.

Shame on all of them, I thought.

See how easily even strangers can steal a spirit?

I committed the light inside me

would never be for sale.

19

∞

Revival

Each morning

the world gets

born again.

How could you not

love mornings?

∞

How Dreams Die

Dreams are gifts

the soul owns

to brighten our darkest days

that get aborted

by fear

      shame

           insecurity.

Do you really want to

kill the soul's gifts?

∞

First Love

I told you I felt as if someone had died

because I couldn't stop crying

while you looked at me with an

expressionless face.

I thought there was something wrong with me

because you didn't react.

You told me to stop crying because it

made me look ugly.

I told you I felt as if someone had died

when I should have felt wonderful

having just told you I loved you

but you said

you didn't love me

and walked away.

My first love

∞

I wonder

Their nests remain

in the corner of the

portale where they

built them last year.

I study the beauty of the

nest's architecture

and wonder

if the birds this year

are the same as last

searching for their

home.

I wonder –

Are these the parents

returning or are these

their children wanting to

sleep in their first beds?

27

∞

Intruder

He was told

how perfect he was

by his mother

who needed an antidote

for her husband's absence.

She wanted him

       dependent

upon her

      always.

So, I left.

When she died

he was in his sixties.

I often wonder –

      How does he live now

          without the two of us?

∞

It wasn't like that years ago

It wasn't like that years ago.

It just wasn't like that.

We knocked on front doors to

talk about springtime

gossip about neighbors

congratulate each other

break up

make up

say witty things

into each other's eyes.

Today we buy devices to

shield us like jackets in the rain

from the mirrors of our souls

complaining about loneliness

with 2069 friends on social media.

As if things weren't tough enough

without another illusion.

Dream

While dreaming in my bed

their screaming voices awakened me

threatening to call an attorney

on each other

in the black of night

cracking peace wide-open.

Today, in my dream,

I see my father's

red and yellow tulips

breaking through garden dirt

as my mother's roast bakes to perfection

and the sun's heat hits

the kitchen window

feigning hope.

In my dreams I kneel at their grave

drape a dozen tulips over their names

let the raw salt of my tears

melt into new grass,

the salty truth of longing

to touch once more.

I have not forgotten.

Awake, I dream for one more -

one more day around the dinner table

one more night with screaming voices

one more chance to lapse into false hope.

Just one more day.

Leaving Brooklyn in 1972

"What does Santa Cruz have
that Brooklyn doesn't?" my mother
wanted to know
the phone limp in my hand.

Where to begin -

Ancient Redwoods
took my sorrow
gave me strength.

Wild horses on Ocean Avenue
took my oppression
seduced me to engage in the wind.

Salty air from ocean breezes
stole my anger
threw me peace from the ocean's depth.

I flew 3,000 miles away to
crack open
a new life.

My mother said I ran away from her.

I said I wanted to go to college.

Yes!

Sometimes
you have to break
your own heart
to be set free.

∞

Light

Would I like my future

if I could see around the corner?

Or, would I want to run

back into the hard times

I just left?

Only one way to find out – so –

here goes –

The next step

into the proverbial dark tunnel

is to enter with faith

and reach for

the light.

∞

Like Whispers

Words caught

between sentences

whispering

the ineffable

stealing darkness from night

like stars

their power

turns over our

hearts.

∞

Listen

The sound of the waves

is the ocean's breath.

In and out.

in and out.

∞

Loneliness

Loneliness is not aloneness.

Loneliness is the absence of joy for solitude.

Find new stories.

      Write a poem.

            Walk in between tall trees.

Smell the aromas of

      honeysuckle

            morning grass.

Listen to

      clapping songs of leaves

            sparrows singing.

Vulnerability becomes your own danger zone

when you forget the soul you share.

∞

To Landon – Just for You

You have inherited

an amazing world.

Look closely.

I have hidden my love

for you in the

beauty of a flower

sweetness of vine-ripened tomatoes

softness of new rain

brilliance of a sunbeam

snap of a freshly baked cookie

foam of tiny ocean waves

sparkle of brilliant stars

radiance of the round moon.

Look closely.

My love is there

waiting -

just for you.

Love

Grandma was German and
served sauerkraut and pork.
There were no secrets hiding
in the air.

Nana was Puerto Rican
had dark skin
served rice and beans
called me Juanita
and drove my parents
into a fury exposing
what they didn't want me to see.

An elusive sense of self
trapped in tabooed curiosity.

"Are we Puerto Rican?"
I once asked my dad.

He left the room
cold beer, unopened, in his
dark hand.

"I don't want my daughter to be called spic."
they whispered in the kitchen.

"I don't want my son with a Puerto Rican from
Brooklyn," my boyfriend's mother
said in the kitchen away
from her son's ears.

In Germany, Hitler's SS soldiers
tortured
tormented
imprisoned
murdered.

In Puerto Rico, people
have joyous passion
love color
feed everyone
care for the land
welcome with warm hugs.

Am I to be
ashamed of being
Puerto Rican?

∞

Morning

Morning makes me jealous

with its lack of agenda

revealing a pure opening with no explanations

no apologies if the weather isn't good

and waits

      for the growth of plants

          birth of insects

              night

to have its time so it can begin again

when the sun rises

over the horizon.

The morning is a blank page.

What will you create today?

∞

Ownership

My father used to smoke Pall Malls
until one day he tired of coughing and
spitting in the early morning
and threw his new pack of smokes
off the roof.

"How can you quit so easily?",
I asked.

"I just decided to," he answered
and taught me how to make
all dreams possible.

One Afternoon in Barnes & Noble

tattoos ringed his neck

ran down his arms

covered his chin

his body donned in black

where the hell is his mother, I asked

staring into a novel

on the sale table

and wondered what I would

do if he were my son

and what father would teach

his boy to get cross-bone tattoos

allow earrings in his nose

and on his face

The tattooed man

moved to a tiny wooden stool

and sat.

A woman dressed in black with

just as many tattoos

placed an infant in his arms

that wore a dress in delicate pink

a small elastic bow hugging

      her tiny head

            holding her

like a blossom holding a bee.

He cooed and ahhhed

softly kissing her cheek,

a vivid smile lightened the baby's face,

her father's angel wings

opened wide.

I collapsed upon myself

folding into my own ugliness

caught in the empty shell

of a woman soberly

wishing he were

her son.

∞

Poems

Poems are eternal.

They are born from echoes of the

      sun's deep edge

           wall's refusal to relent

                lock's lost key

     heart's sharp fragment

                    wave's arrogant roar

in the journey.

A poem plucks her roots

from the invisible voice

shakes her soul

cracks it open

caustic as a

raw onion.

Promises

I'm not like them

he said

      those other men you dated

I'm not like them

he said

blue eyes

curtains to the sun.

He was right --

my possessions started missing

night lights turned off

desert dirt left on the

floor I washed in early morning

skylights used for his abuse.

I'm not like them

he chanted forcing many

court dates

orders of protection

stalking

sabotaging safety.

The Bible says

God sees everything -

even a pair of

blue eyes

breaking

solemn promises.

∞

Restless

The mind keeps us
awake at night when
darkness is supposed
to let us rest for a new
day.

Twisting and turning
fighting our minds
to forget the unforgettable

until we pay attention.

Reality

A simple vision -

        know life's meaning

            know life's purpose

build a direct plan for success

no need to waste time

looking inward

no need to know

just follow my *will*

how hard can it be?

Ha!

This life-road is messy,

muddy, insane,

obscures meaning

waylays defined plans

provides no answers

fails often

births existential angst

teases the power of control

disables the will

      replete with vulnerability

pulsates anger

scratches peace

forces the unknown

to meet eye to eye

overriding will

everything seemingly planned

beyond human control.

Reality is not

what we think it is.

Right Where I Am

I decided many decades ago
that everything in my life is
a series of lessons.

I've had to let go of people I
wanted to hold onto
and thought I couldn't
survive the pain of their loss -
but I did.

I entered my aloneness
and found God there
waiting
just when I thought I had
been abandoned.

Everything has a reason.
I don't always know what it is.
I ask how much more
Can my broken heart take?

I look up to see

     a sunrise

         a star

            a butterfly

               receive a smile.

And am reassured

that I belong right where I am.

∞

Roads

I love walking on dirt roads in sandals

to slide my toes into its dust.

The earth holds so much power

ready for seeds

to sprout life.

To cover the dirt with concrete

is to deny mother earth her voice

to stop the heartbeat that connects to ours

nurturing us with her constant

love and creativity.

We have to stop oppressing

the earth's

muse.

∞

Roses

Two tiny rose bushes

sit on my table

one is dead

one is alive

      life and death.

I watered and cared for

them the same.

Isn't that how life is?

One dies

another lives

lost in mystery.

∞

Salt

He presses down on the few particulates of
salt fallen onto the table with his index
finger, as if declaring,

I am here, I am here!

∞

Santa Fe Mountains

The Santa Fe Mountains release a sigh

into the breath of a sunrise

from a long night

of exposing their strength

to the moon.

They hold the earth's secrets

as the birds fly south

for the winter

and the pinion grows stronger.

∞

Sessions

They come to see me

one by one.

I ask where

their pain is

and help them

listen.

∞

Stardust

I heard a scientist say that we

are made of stardust.

I loved that thought

and hung on

his every word.

The taste delicious -

       I am made of the universe.

           I am all of it.

               I am everything.

                    I am the light of stars.

Now I have scientific proof –

who I am.

∞

The Destination

I buried my father

in Brooklyn on

a rainy day in August

and pretended the two

overweight cemetery workers

were sliding his casket

into a subway car

a single rose thrown on top

to send him

to a town where he could

dance and laugh and

eat his favorite foods

in order to believe

he would enjoy his new

destination.

∞

The Hug

My grandmother's apartment

sat above a restaurant called The Kabin.

She lived there alone.

When I visited, I had to climb

two steep staircases.

She always awaited

      eagerly

for my arrival

      at her opened door

            dishtowel in hand

                  apron dusted with baking flour

scooping me in her arms

      pressing me against her soft bosoms with a

          warm embrace.

Not even my mother hugged me like that.

Not even my mother hugged me.

∞

Travels

She asked me where I traveled and
I told her.

          around the sharp edges of hope

          into the black centers of fear

          into the redness of anger

          around the eternal presence of death

          into the pink newness of relationship adventures

          into the claustrophobic crack of un unrequited love

          into the blueness of abandonment

          into the greyness of homelessness

          into the greenness of wealth

          into the redness of poverty

          into the whiteness of the divine

          into the purpose of wholeness

Her eyes rounded.

I've only been to France, she nervously giggled.

81

∞

Truth

We have this illusion, you and I, that
we are setting down roots with our buildings
but we are roaming, just roaming.

The walls are fake
there are no walls in our lives.
The ground is an illusion - there is no ground.
Our souls float and swim and press forward
thinking we are handling our journey
but we cannot handle such a journey.

The joke is on us, we will soon learn, because
it is all ineffable, this journey we call life.

The walls, the cement, and the ground are not made
by God but by our fears that we will perish if we
live in the air and trees and on the sea.

You cannot abandon God and build anything real.

∞

Two Words

Two words

scare the muse

sending her to write with

passion

and fury:

published

posthumously

∞

Viera

The pen stops, then touches the whiteness

of the page's horizon and I take in a

breath that freezes in midair.

My lungs fill but I can't exhale.

I'm afraid I'll disappear with my own breath

as I try to write about your failing body and our

decades of friendship

as you lay on a

high mattress with your two children on either side.

I was too sick to fly to the coast to say

goodbye and knew something in me

would die with you and never come back.

∞

Voices

Trees whisper

like a mother reading

bedtime stories

awakening something inside me

to paste on the unmarked pages

of a memoir

proof

that I have lived at least

this one moment well.

∞

What if . . .

An ad in the personals read:
"I know this is silly but I'm dying and
I want to find love before I die. If you want
to take a chance let me know."

I reached for the phone several times.
My heart breaking.
Could my heart take another loss?
The receiver stayed nestled in the phone.

But . . .
What if he hadn't died?
What if our love had healed him?
What if one day we were to sit on the porch sipping wine
laughing at the risk we took
that turned our lives around?

It's been thirty-five years.

I still wonder -
What if. . .

∞

What is a Lover?

Tell me – what is a lover?

Is it someone who thrills with touches and tickles in the night's darkness?

Is it someone who, under cool sheets, lets his heart beat in synchronization with love promises?

Or is it someone who says,

"I will always be there for you. I will hold you and yet set you free."

then lights up every time you enter a room?

∞

which way

 am I a gypsy facing stars

with no direction

waiting for a sign

for which way to go

waiting for God

watching the tides

listening to the sages

and proceeding just the same

∞

Who Will You Become?

A grey caterpillar with

white spots crawled in front of me as I read on a large

rock in the sun.

I dreamed of what kind of

butterfly it would

become, just as, I suspect,

my parents dreamed of what kind of

woman I would become.

Wisdom Deferred

When I was young I used to

count the years on my fingers

to figure out how many were left until

I didn't have to go to school anymore.

Then I finally

graduated high school.

No more homework.

No more tests.

No more kids teasing me.

I got a good job on

Wall Street and made money and

thought I was successful at last.

But my world became too

small and I longed to make it

bigger so I looked into going

back to school.

At 65

I count the years on my fingers

that might remain

to live my one wild and valuable life

to see if there is enough time to

get another degree

fulfill more dreams

as the flowers

bloom and my friends

die of different causes.

∞

Without Death

He watches

the woman with

shoulder length earrings

her lover by her side

scratch their names

with different pens

into his shop's table.

They walk out

with drinks untouched

remembering the time

he and his girlfriend

scratched names

into a table

on their way to sign

their marriage license.

Without Permission

Unnoticed
life slides its way
through the heart
sneaking into places we
know not
then escapes
again unnoticed.

Catastrophes show no discrimination
nor do they promise to destroy.
Love shows no discrimination
nor does it promise to save.

Do you see?

A baby's cry
stomach's growl
politician's plea
newlywed's dream

another day

is given and taken away

so easily

without permission

just the strong assertion

of the breath's fragility.

∞

Your Way

I love you, I said in each phone call

my plea

to force you to stop hurting yourself.

I need you not to die, I said

but you ignored me and

did whatever you wanted

and pushed my love away

convinced

you were unloved.

You died holding onto

your belief.

You died

the way you lived,

refusing to

believe

how much you were

      loved

while the cold set in and we dropped

roses on your grave.

Hot Rock

I sit on a large hot white rock

baked by the Texas sun

resting on a bed of grass

surrounded by trees intermingling

in staunch cooperation

on this sunny day when I want to read

outside.

Today is glorious!

Busy ants climb on the pages

of May Sarton's poetry about nature's

light.

A blue dragonfly lands next to

me as if knowing I want company while

I read.

Gnats in cameo appearances turn and

quickly fly away.

How can anyone be lonely?

Life is everywhere?

∞

A Full Life

They rolled in on wheelchairs

with sunken faces

dead eyes

tired

aching

hunched over backs

stiff spines

remembering the days

they carried babies

washed clothes

bought groceries

blew out birthday candles

washed floors

made money and love

now only memories

of a full life.

A Love Story

I met a roach on my floor
and tried to slide it in a jar
but it ran faster than I could catch
soon vanishing under the carpet.

A flash of an old memory hit hard
"you almost died," a nurse said
to me 28 years ago.

The roach reappeared.
I fought it hard to get it into the
old mayonnaise jar
the beauty of its
burnt red skin, quick legs, solid body
working overtime.

 "There is food for you outside," I said
capturing it and
hurrying outside to
tilt the glass jar to free it
to the ground where it quickly
took off, turned,
then raced back towards me.

"No," I insisted. "You must go another way,"
and pointed to the grass.

Like a child not wanting to be separated
from its mother it ran to my foot.

Like a mother sending a child to its
first day of school
I rushed into the house
quickly shutting the door.

∞

A New Friend

I sat in the weak sun reading May Sarton

on the steps behind my apartment.

Grief for the loss of a

friend, one month older than me,

ravaged my mood and stole me from the words

I was trying to read.

A rustle in the bush stole the moment.

Sauntering slowly

a large majestic buck

walked in front

of me, ate leaves, waved his

strong and dramatic antlers

in the air.

One friend lost.

Another gained.

∞

A Simple Man

"What are your dreams?"

I asked my father

because Oprah

said it was a good idea to ask.

"Dreams?"

"Yes, tell me."

"I am a simple man.

     I go to work.

          I come home.

               I take care of my family," he said

falling asleep in the sun.

I buried him

deep below the grass

longing to ask him for

his stories, the ones that

held his life together.

 "Stories?" he would have said.

     "I am a simple man."

∞

Alligator

What makes the alligator so angry

that he won't let you get close?

What is it about the alligator

that nature has had to adapt

his teeth and muscles to be so

strong so no one would

fall in love with him?

I think I might be an alligator.

An Unexpected Murder

A tickle like a bird's feather

kissed my naked ankle

on my first day

in the New Mexico desert

ill and fearing for my life.

It was a dark black stink bug struggling

to climb my leg

desiring higher ground.

I nudged it into a tea cup as

it lifted its butt and emitted a

bitter aroma in fear.

"I won't hurt you," I said

and took it where the sun could

warm its thinly ribbed back

to crawl onto the land

it knew better than me.

On another day a stranger

walked onto my property

to ask a question

as the stink bug approached

possibly to offer the man a

welcoming tickle that comforted my morning

that first day my new life in the desert

was about to unfold.

He lifted his heavy boot and

laid it heavily upon its

back.

"Get off my land," I yelled. *"Get off! Get off!"*

Stunned, he asked, "Why? What did I do?"

"You killed that beautiful creature. What did the

stink bug ever do to you?"

 He looked at me in disgust.

"It's just a *bug*," he announced.

"No," I retorted, "it is not *just* a bug. It is a stink bug

with a name just like you and me.

It is life. It is breath. It is kinder than you."

119

He laughed.

"Get off my land," I yelled

and knew that the path for my healing

was love.

Blossoms Aren't Late

I used to say I was a late bloomer
as I sat waiting for you
in a state of *meantime*
and busied myself with things
of passion.

In my 60's
my petals have turned to compost
I think I am re-born
having blossomed after all.

Azalea

My father planted a vibrant pink azalea

in our front yard

a gift to my mother for their anniversary -

its radiant pink blossoms pushed delicately

into the air

in compact abundance

announcing the advent of spring.

Passersby stopped to stare

cameras in hand to take

pictures of the stunning beauty

that took over the yard each year.

Oh, how they loved to watch that azalea

give birth to spring year after year.

Another family enjoys it now

and watches the azalea push forth its blossoms

--or maybe –

passersby no longer fall

in love with my memories.

Be Self-Taught

Go ahead and

listen to others bark on

about

       what they know

          how they think

in this vast and troubled

amazing and changing

world.

Take it all in.

But know too that your journey

inside your heart that

speaks to your

heartache and sickness

laughter and grief

love and beauty

success and missed opportunities

can only teach you their

meanings for your life.

Learn your own wisdom.

∞

Betrayal Unrecognized

the creek is busy with activity

trees whisper in the breeze

grasses clap

mosquitoes kiss the water

centering the moment

but --

far away

elephants scream

rhinos run

polar bears drown

where will we be able to hide

from fallen

consciousness

Unexpected Life

I had a small birdbath in my courtyard when I lived in the
desert and watched birds with unknown names drink and
bathe alongside each other.

Moths with charcoal backs the size of hands revealed pristine
white wings decorated with a golf-ball sized vivid orange dot;
sage green moths, tiny and delicate as yesterday's lace; and
black, white, and pink striped crickets resembling Good n'
Plenty candies visited every day.

In a corner against the adobe wall, a horny toad lizard
crawled out of a small mud cave
its blue and green horny back
so beautiful I couldn't catch myself before
I broke out in joyous tears
and watched a lizard with a canary
yellow tail dart into a bush to chase a fly
in amazing surprise.

Bull snakes, red racer snakes, green pencil-thinned garter snakes and dozens more slithered against my walls, into my garage, and played with rabbits out for the hunt.

New born bunnies no bigger than a tennis ball exited small holes in the dirt growing to the size of dogs who jumped across my land under skies of orange, blue, green, yellow, purple, black and blue.

Everything taught me that living in the dessert was going to require respect for all God's creatures instead of seeing that which I didn't understand as the enemy.

My friend, Norman, the poet, asked me why I moved to a place with so much dirt. I sent him a list of the life I discovered.

Norman, I said,
I hardly notice the dirt.

∞

Howling

The wind is the desert's voice.

Its voice hard and angry
like a lion in the jungle declaring
its territory.

For days it howled
until I wanted to scream for it
to stop and give me peace
remembering the stories of cowboys who used to go
insane from the sound of the wind.

"You must know," the wind speaks
"that only I am
Goddess of the desert."

∞

Pen

He made a pen for me out of

spiral koa.

I write with it

every day.

It nurtures me.

It makes me think I'm

writing with a branch.

But I ask . . .

What happened to the rest

of the tree?

Any work of art makes one very simple demand on anyone who genuinely wants to get in touch with it. And that is to stop. You've got to stop what you're doing, what you're thinking, and what you're expecting and just be there for the poem for however long it takes.

W. S. Merwin

Let everything happen to you

Beauty and terror

Just keep going

No feeling is final

Rainer Maria Rilke

Write your poems here:

Write your poems here:

Write your poems here:

Write your poems here:

About the Author

Jan Marquart is a licensed clinical social worker, educator, author, and dynamic motivational speaker.

She has authored 24 books and has been published in local newspapers in New Mexico and California. She has received the National Self-Published Book Award for 2000 from *Writers Digest* for her memoir, *The Breath of Dawn, A Journey of Everyday Blessings,* and received the Editor's Choice Award from the International Library of Poetry for her poem, "Yesterday."

Her poems, essays, stories, and creative non-fiction pieces have been published online at: www.everywritersresource.com, Poetry Victims, www.ladyinkmagazine.com, Solecisms, IndianaVoiceJournal.com, Scars Publications (Down in the Dirt), and others.

Most writers have a niche in which they write. Jan enjoys trying her pen in all genres. Her muse is constantly dancing to different tunes.

She teaches The Provocation of Journal Writing, Write Short – Write Deep and What Is It Like to Be Your Mother's Daughter? for Life Learning Institute, an organization whose classes specialize for those over 50. She also teaches therapeutic writing for Story Circle Network, an international women's writing circle.

Her blog is:
www.freethepen.wordpress.com

Her websites are:
www.JanMarquart.com
www.CanYouFindMyLove.com
www.AwareLivingNow.Blogspot.com

All her books can be ordered on:
www.JanMarquart.com.
Amazon.com
Barnes&Noble.com

www.ingramcontent.com/pod-product-compliance
Lightning Source LLC
Chambersburg PA
CBHW032004040426
42448CB00006B/478